ALUMINUM CROCHET HOOKS

UNITED STATES	METRIC (mm)
B-1	2.25
C-2	2.75
D-3	3.25
E-4	3.50
F-5	3.75
G-6	4.00
H-8	5.00
I-9	5.50
J-10	6.00
K-10½	6.50
N	9.00
P	10.00
Q	15.00

STEEL CROCHET HOOKS

UNITED STATES	METRIC (mm)
00	3.50
0	3.25
1	2.75
2	2.25
3	2.10
4	2.00
5	1.90
6	1.80
7	1.65
8	1.50
9	1.40
10	1.30
11	1.10
12	1.00
13	0.85
14	0.75

or in ....c.y a guide and should never be used without first making a sample swatch approximately 4" square in the stitch, yarn, and hook specified. Then measure the swatch, counting your stitches and rows carefully. If your swatch is larger or smaller than specified, **make another, changing hook size to get the correct gauge**. Keep trying until you find the size hook that will give you the specified gauge.

JOINING WITH SC

When instructed to join with sc, begin with a slip knot on hook. Insert hook in stitch or space indicated, YO and pull up a loop, YO and draw through both loops on hook.

FREE LOOPS OF A CHAIN

When instructed to work in free loops of a chain, work in loop indicated by arrow *(Fig. 1)*.

Fig. 1

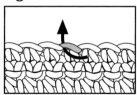

We have made every effort to ensure that these instructions are accurate and complete. We cannot, however, be responsible for human error, typographical mistakes, or variations in individual work.

BACK RIDGE

Work only in loops indicated by arrows *(Fig. 2)*.

Fig. 2

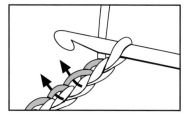

BACK LOOP ONLY

Work only in loop(s) indicated by arrow *(Fig. 3)*.

Fig. 3

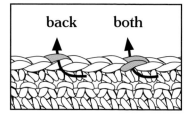

1. SWEET DREAMS AFGHAN

Shown on page 13.

Finished Size:
35" x 41"

MATERIALS

Baby Fingering Weight Yarn:
11 ounces,
(310 grams, 1,695 yards)
Steel crochet hook, size 3 (2.10 mm) **or** size needed for gauge

GAUGE: In pattern, (sc, ch 4, dc) 7 times and 13 rows = 4"

AFGHAN BODY

Ch 188 **loosely**.

Row 1 (Right side)**:** Sc in eighth ch from hook, ★ ch 4, skip next 3 chs, sc in next ch; repeat from ★ across: 46 sps.

Row 2: Ch 5, turn; (sc, ch 4, dc) in first ch-4 sp, ch 1, ★ (sc, ch 4, dc) in next ch-4 sp, ch 1; repeat from ★ across to last sp, sc in last sp: 45 ch-4 sps and one ch-5 sp.

To work Shell, (hdc, dc, ch 1, dc, hdc) in sp indicated.

Row 3: Ch 5, turn; skip first ch-1 sp, (sc, ch 4, dc) in next ch-4 sp, ch 1, ★ work Shell in next ch-4 sp, ch 1, (sc, ch 4, dc) in next ch-4 sp, ch 1; repeat from ★ across to last ch-5 sp, sc in last ch-5 sp: 23 ch-4 sps, 22 Shells, and one ch-5 sp.

Row 4: Ch 5, turn; skip first ch-1 sp, (sc, ch 4, dc) in next ch-4 sp, ch 1, ★ skip next ch-1 sp, (sc, ch 4, dc) in next Shell (ch-1 sp), ch 1, (sc, ch 4, dc) in next ch-4 sp, ch 1; repeat from ★ across to last ch-5 sp, sc in last ch-5 sp: 45 ch-4 sps and one ch-5 sp.

Row 5: Ch 5, turn; skip first ch-1 sp, work Shell in next ch-4 sp, ch 1, ★ (sc, ch 4, dc) in next ch-4 sp, ch 1, work Shell in next ch-4 sp, ch 1; repeat from ★ across to last ch-5 sp, sc in last ch-5 sp: 22 ch-4 sps, 23 Shells, and one ch-5 sp.

Row 6: Ch 5, turn; skip first ch-1 sp, (sc, ch 4, dc) in next Shell, ch 1, ★ (sc, ch 4, dc) in next ch-4 sp, ch 1, (sc, ch 4, dc) in next Shell, ch 1; repeat from ★ across to last ch-5 sp, sc in last ch-5 sp: 45 ch-4 sps and one ch-5 sp.

Rows 7-106: Repeat Rows 3-6, 25 times; do **not** finish off.

EDGING

Rnd 1: Ch 1, turn; skip first ch-1 sp and slip st in next ch-4 sp, ch 1, (sc, ch 4, dc) in same sp, ch 1, [(sc, ch 4, dc) in next ch-4 sp, ch 1] across to last ch-5 sp, (sc, ch 6, dc, ch 1, sc, ch 4, dc) in last ch-5 sp, ch 1; working in ch-5 sps at end of rows, [(sc, ch 4, dc) in next ch-5 sp, ch 1] across; working in sps over beginning ch, (sc, ch 6, dc, ch 1, sc, ch 4, dc) in first sp, ch 1, [(sc, ch 4, dc) in next sp, ch 1] across to last sp, (sc, ch 6, dc, ch 1, sc, ch 4, dc) in last sp, ch 1; working in ch-5 sps at end of rows, [(sc, ch 4, dc) in next ch-5 sp, ch 1] across, (sc, ch 6, dc) in same sp as first sc, ch 1; join with slip st to first sc: 196 ch-4 sps and 4 ch-6 sps.

To work treble crochet *(abbreviated tr)*, YO twice, insert hook in sp indicated, YO and pull up a loop (4 loops on hook), (YO and draw through 2 loops on hook) 3 times.

Rnd 2: Ch 1, turn; skip first ch-1 sp and slip st in next ch-6 sp, ch 6 **(counts as first tr plus ch 2)**, (tr in same sp, ch 2) twice, sc in next ch-4 sp, ch 2, ★ † (hdc, ch 1, dc) in next ch-4 sp, ch 2, [tr, (ch 1, tr) twice] in next ch-4 sp, ch 2, (dc, ch 1, hdc) in next ch-4 sp, ch 2, sc in next ch-4 sp, ch 2 †, repeat from † to † across to next corner ch-6 sp, (tr, ch 2) 3 times in corner ch-6 sp, sc in next ch-4 sp, ch 2; repeat from ★ 2 times **more**, then repeat from † to † across; join with slip st to first tr: 52 3-tr groups.

To work sp decrease *(uses next 2 sps)*, ★ YO, insert hook in **next** sp, YO and pull up a loop, YO and draw through 2 loops on hook; repeat from ★ once **more**, YO and draw through all 3 loops on hook **(counts as one dc)**.

Rnd 3: Ch 4 **(counts as first dc plus ch 1)**, turn; ★ dc in next ch-2 sp, work sp decrease, ch 1, dc in next dc, ch 1, dc in next ch-2 sp and in next tr, ch 1, 3 dc in next tr, ch 1, dc in next tr and in next ch-2 sp, ch 1, dc in next dc, ch 1, † work sp decrease twice, ch 1, dc in next dc, ch 1, dc in next ch-2 sp and in next tr, ch 1, 3 dc in next tr, ch 1, dc in next tr and in next ch-2 sp, ch 1, dc in next dc, ch 1 †, repeat from † to † 9 times **more**, work sp decrease, dc in next ch-2 sp, ch 1, dc in next tr and in next ch-2 sp, ch 1, 3 dc in next tr, ch 1, dc in next ch-2 sp and in next tr, ch 1, dc in next ch-2 sp, work sp decrease, ch 1, dc in next dc, ch 1, dc in next ch-2 sp and in next tr, ch 1, 3 dc in next tr, ch 1, dc in next tr and in next ch-2 sp, ch 1, dc in next dc, ch 1, repeat from † to † 12 times, work sp decrease, dc in next ch-2 sp, ch 1, dc in next tr and in next ch-2 sp, ch 1, 3 dc in next tr, ch 1 ★, dc in next ch-2 sp and in next tr, ch 1, repeat from ★ to ★ once, dc in last ch-2 sp; join with slip st to first dc: 868 sts.

To work st decrease, YO, insert hook in **next** st, YO and pull up a loop, YO and draw through 2 loops on hook, YO, skip next ch, insert hook in **next** st, YO and pull up a loop, YO and draw through 2 loops on hook, YO and draw through all 3 loops on hook (**counts as one dc**).

Rnd 4: Ch 3 (**counts as first dc, now and throughout**), turn; dc in next 3 sts, ★ 3 dc in next dc, dc in next 6 sts, work st decrease, dc in next 5 sts, 3 dc in next dc, dc in next 5 sts, † work st decrease twice, dc in next 5 sts, 3 dc in next dc, dc in next 5 sts †, repeat from † to † 11 times **more**, work st decrease, dc in next 6 sts, 3 dc in next dc, dc in next 6 sts, work st decrease, dc in next 5 sts, 3 dc in next dc, dc in next 5 sts, repeat from † to † 10 times, work st decrease ★, dc in next 6 sts, repeat from ★ to ★ once, dc in last 2 sts; join with slip st to first dc: 780 dc.

Rnd 5: Ch 3, turn; dc in next dc, ★ † skip next 2 dc, dc in next 6 dc, ch 1, dc in next dc, ch 1, dc in next 6 dc †, repeat from † to † 10 times **more**, skip next 2 dc, dc in next 5 dc, ch 1, (dc in next dc, ch 1) 3 times, dc in next 5 dc, repeat from † to † 13 times, skip next 2 dc, dc in next 5 dc, ch 1, (dc in next dc, ch 1) 3 times ★, dc in next 5 dc, repeat from ★ to ★ once, dc in last 3 dc; join with slip st to first dc: 676 dc and 112 ch-1 sps.

Rnd 6: Ch 3, turn; dc in next 3 dc, ★ ch 1, dc in next ch-1 sp, ch 1, dc in next dc, ch 1, dc in next ch-1 sp, dc in next dc and in next ch-1 sp, ch 1, dc in next dc, ch 1, dc in next ch-1 sp, ch 1, dc in next 5 dc, skip next dc, dc in next 5 dc and in next ch-1 sp, ch 1, dc in next dc, ch 1, dc in next ch-1 sp and in next 5 dc, † skip next 2 dc, dc in next 5 dc and in next ch-1 sp, ch 1, dc in next dc, ch 1, dc in next ch-1 sp and in next 5 dc †, repeat from † to † 11 times **more**, skip next dc, dc in next 5 dc, ch 1, dc in next ch-1 sp, ch 1, dc in next dc, ch 1, dc in next ch-1 sp, dc in next dc and in next ch-1 sp, ch 1, dc in next dc, ch 1, dc in next ch-1 sp, ch 1, dc in next 5 dc, skip next dc, dc in next 5 dc and in next ch-1 sp, ch 1, dc in next dc, ch 1, dc in next ch-1 sp and in next 5 dc, repeat from † to † 10 times, skip next dc ★, dc in next 5 dc, repeat from ★ to ★ once, dc in last dc; join with slip st to first dc: 692 dc and 120 ch-1 sps.

Rnd 7: Ch 3, turn; ★ † skip next 2 dc, dc in next 5 dc and in next ch-1 sp, ch 1, dc in next dc, ch 1, dc in next ch-1 sp and in next 5 dc †, repeat from † to † 10 times **more**, skip next 2 dc, dc in next 4 dc, dc in next ch-1 sp and in next dc, ch 1, dc in next ch-1 sp, ch 1, dc in next dc, dc in next ch-1 sp and in next 3 dc, dc in next ch-1 sp and in next dc, ch 1, dc in next ch-1 sp, ch 1, dc in next dc, dc in next ch-1 sp and in next 4 dc, repeat from † to † 13 times, skip next 2 dc, dc in next 4 dc, dc in next ch-1 sp and in next dc, ch 1, dc in next ch-1 sp, ch 1, dc in next dc, dc in next ch-1 sp and in next 3 dc, dc in next ch-1 sp and in next dc, ch 1, dc in next ch-1 sp, ch 1, dc in next dc and in next ch-1 sp ★, dc in next 4 dc, repeat from ★ to ★ once, dc in last 3 dc; join with slip st to first dc: 708 dc and 112 ch-1 sps.

Rnd 8: Turn; slip st in next dc, ch 3, dc in next 4 dc and in next ch-1 sp, ★ ch 1, dc in next dc, ch 1, dc in next ch-1 sp, dc in next 7 dc and in next ch-1 sp, ch 1, dc in next dc, ch 1, dc in next ch-1 sp and in next 5 dc, † skip next 2 dc, dc in next 5 dc and in next ch-1 sp, ch 1, dc in next dc, ch 1, dc in next ch-1 sp and in next 5 dc †, repeat from † to † 12 times **more**, skip next 2 dc, dc in next 5 dc and in next ch-1 sp, ch 1, dc in next dc, ch 1, dc in next ch-1 sp, dc in next 7 dc and in next ch-1 sp, ch 1, dc in next dc, ch 1, dc in next ch-1 sp and in next 5 dc, repeat from † to † 11 times ★, skip next 2 dc, dc in next 5 dc and in next ch-1 sp, repeat from ★ to ★ once, skip last 2 sts; join with slip st to first dc: 716 dc.

Rnd 9: Slip st in next dc, ch 3, **turn**; ★ skip next 2 sts, dc in next 5 dc and in next ch-1 sp, ch 1, dc in next dc, ch 1, † dc in next ch-1 sp and in next 5 dc, skip next 2 dc, dc in next 5 dc and in next ch-1 sp, ch 1, dc in next dc, ch 1 †, repeat from † to † 10 times **more**, dc in next ch-1 sp and in next 3 dc, skip next dc, (dc, ch 1, dc) in next dc, skip next dc, dc in next 3 dc and in next ch-1 sp, ch 1, dc in next dc, ch 1, repeat from † to † 14 times, dc in next ch-1 sp and in next 3 dc, skip next dc, (dc, ch 1, dc) in next dc, skip next dc, dc in next 3 dc and in next ch-1 sp, ch 1, dc in next dc, ch 1 ★, dc in next ch-1 sp and in next 5 dc, repeat from ★ to ★ once, dc in next ch-1 sp and in last 4 dc; join with slip st to first dc: 720 dc and 116 ch-1 sps.

Rnd 10: Turn; slip st in next dc, ch 3, dc in next 4 dc and in next ch-1 sp, ch 1, dc in next dc, ch 1, ★ dc in next ch-1 sp and in next 4 dc, skip next dc, (dc, ch 1, dc) in next ch-1 sp, skip next dc, dc in next 4 dc and in next ch-1 sp, ch 1, dc in next dc, ch 1, † dc in next ch-1 sp and in next 5 dc, skip next 2 dc, dc in next 5 dc and in next ch-1 sp, ch 1, dc in next dc, ch 1 †, repeat from † to † 13 times **more**, dc in next ch-1 sp and in next 4 dc, skip next dc, (dc, ch 1, dc) in next ch-1 sp, skip next dc, dc in next 4 dc and in next ch-1 sp, ch 1, dc in

next dc, ch 1 ★, repeat from † to † 12 times, repeat from ★ to ★ once, then repeat from † to † 11 times, dc in next ch-1 sp and in next 5 dc, skip last 2 sts; join with slip st to first dc: 728 dc.

Rnd 11: Slip st in next dc, ch 3, **turn**; ★ † skip next 2 sts, dc in next 5 dc and in next ch-1 sp, ch 1, dc in next dc, ch 1, dc in next ch-1 sp and in next 5 dc †, repeat from † to † 11 times **more**, skip next dc, dc in next ch-1 sp, (ch 1, dc in same sp) twice, skip next dc, dc in next 5 dc and in next ch-1 sp, ch 1, dc in next dc, ch 1, dc in next ch-1 sp and in next 5 dc, repeat from † to † 14 times, skip next dc, dc in next ch-1 sp, (ch 1, dc in same sp) twice, skip next dc, dc in next 5 dc and in next ch-1 sp, ch 1, dc in next dc, ch 1 ★, dc in next ch-1 sp and in next 5 dc, repeat from ★ to ★ once, dc in next ch-1 sp and in last 4 dc; join with slip st to first dc: 740 dc and 120 ch-1 sps.

Rnd 12: Turn; slip st in next dc, ch 3, dc in next 4 dc and in next ch-1 sp, ch 1, dc in next dc, ch 1, dc in next ch-1 sp and in next 5 dc, ★ skip next dc, dc in next dc, (ch 1, dc in next ch-1 sp, ch 1, dc in next dc) twice, skip next dc, dc in next 5 dc and in next ch-1 sp, ch 1, dc in next dc, ch 1, dc in next ch-1 sp and in next 5 dc, † skip next 2 dc, dc in next 5 dc and in next ch-1 sp, ch 1, dc in next dc, ch 1, dc in next ch-1 sp and in next 5 dc †, repeat from † to † 13 times **more**, skip next dc, dc in next dc, (ch 1, dc in next ch-1 sp, ch 1, dc in next dc) twice, skip next dc, dc in next 5 dc and in next ch-1 sp, ch 1, dc in next dc, ch 1, dc in next ch-1 sp and in next 5 dc ★, repeat from † to † 12 times, repeat from ★ to ★ once, then repeat from † to † 11 times, skip last 2 sts; join with slip st to first dc: 748 dc and 128 ch-1 sps.

Rnd 13: Slip st in next dc, ch 3, **turn**; ★ † skip next 2 sts, dc in next 3 dc, [skip next st, (dc, ch 1, dc) in next dc] 3 times, skip next dc, dc in next 3 dc †, repeat from † to † 11 times **more**, skip next dc, dc in next dc, [skip next ch-1 sp, (dc, ch 1, dc) in next dc] 3 times, skip next ch-1 sp, dc in next dc, skip next dc, dc in next 3 dc, [skip next st, (dc, ch 1, dc) in next dc] 3 times, skip next dc, dc in next 3 dc, repeat from † to † 14 times, skip next dc, dc in next dc, [skip next ch-1 sp, (dc, ch 1, dc) in next dc] 3 times, skip next ch-1 sp, dc in next dc, skip next dc, dc in next 3 dc, [skip next st, (dc, ch 1, dc) in next dc] 3 times, skip next dc ★, dc in next 3 dc, repeat from ★ to ★ once, dc in last 2 dc; join with slip st to first dc: 704 dc and 180 ch-1 sps.

To work Picot, ch 3, slip st in top of last dc made.

Rnd 14: Slip st in next 2 dc, ch 1, do **not** turn; sc in same st, ch 2, sc in next dc, ch 2, (sc, ch 3) twice in next ch-1 sp, (dc, work Picot, dc) in next ch-1 sp, (ch 3, sc) twice in next ch-1 sp, ch 2, † skip next dc, sc in next dc, ch 2, sc in next dc, ch 1, skip next 2 dc, (sc in next dc, ch 2) twice, (sc, ch 3) twice in next ch-1 sp, (dc, work Picot, dc) in next ch-1 sp, (ch 3, sc) twice in next ch-1 sp, ch 2 †, repeat from † to † 10 times **more**, ★ skip next 2 dc, sc in next dc, ch 2, skip next dc, sc in next dc, ch 2, (sc, ch 3) twice in next ch-1 sp, (dc, work Picot, dc) in next ch-1 sp, (ch 3, sc) twice in next ch-1 sp, ch 2, (skip next dc, sc in next dc, ch 2) twice, (sc, ch 3) twice in next ch-1 sp, (dc, work Picot, dc) in next ch-1 sp, (ch 3, sc) twice in next ch-1 sp, ch 2, repeat from † to † 14 times, skip next 2 dc, sc in next dc, ch 2, skip next dc, sc in next dc, ch 2, (sc, ch 3) twice in next ch-1 sp, (dc, work Picot, dc) in next ch-1 sp, (ch 3, sc) twice in next ch-1 sp, ch 2, (skip next dc, sc in next dc, ch 2) twice, (sc, ch 3) twice in next ch-1 sp, (dc, work Picot, dc) in next ch-1 sp, (ch 3, sc) twice in next ch-1 sp, ch 2 ★, repeat from † to † 12 times, then repeat from ★ to ★ once, skip next dc, sc in next dc, ch 2, sc in next dc, ch 1, skip last 2 sts; join with slip st to first sc, finish off.

Design by Carol Decker.

2. PRETTY PUFFS AFGHAN

Shown on Back Cover.

Finished Size:
36" x 45"

MATERIALS

Sport Weight Yarn:
16 ounces,
(450 grams, 1,600 yards)
Crochet hook, size G (4.00 mm)
or size needed for gauge

GAUGE: In pattern,
one repeat and Rows 1-9 = 5"

AFGHAN BODY

Ch 108 **loosely**.

Row 1: Sc in second ch from hook, skip next ch, (sc, ch 2, sc) in next ch, ch 3, skip next 3 chs, dc in next ch, ch 3, (skip next 2 chs, dc in next ch, ch 3) twice, skip next 3 chs, (sc, ch 2, sc) in next ch, ★ ch 1, skip next 2 chs, sc in next ch, ch 3, skip next ch, sc in next ch, ch 1, skip next 2 chs, (sc, ch 2, sc) in next ch, ch 3, skip next 3 chs, dc in next ch, ch 3, (skip next 2 chs, dc in next ch, ch 3) twice, skip next 3 chs, (sc, ch 2, sc) in next ch; repeat from ★ across to last 2 chs, skip next ch, sc in last ch: 42 sps.

To work V-St, (dc, ch 2, dc) in sp indicated.

To work Puff St, ★ YO, insert hook in sp indicated, YO and pull up a loop even with last st made; repeat from ★ 2 times **more**, YO and draw through first 6 loops on hook, YO and draw through remaining 2 loops on hook.

Row 2 (Right side)**:** Ch 3 **(counts as first dc, now and throughout)**, turn; work V-St in next ch-2 sp, ch 2, dc in next ch-3 sp, ch 2, sc in next ch-3 sp, ch 3, sc in next ch-3 sp, ch 2, dc in next ch-3 sp, ch 2, work V-St in next ch-2 sp, ★ skip next ch-1 sp, work (Puff St, ch 3, Puff St) in next ch-3 sp, skip next ch-1 sp, work V-St in next ch-2 sp, ch 2, dc in next ch-3 sp, ch 2, sc in next ch-3 sp, ch 3, sc in next ch-3 sp, ch 2, dc in next ch-3 sp, ch 2, work V-St in next ch-2 sp; repeat from ★ across to last 2 sc, skip next sc, dc in last sc: 39 sps.

Row 3: Ch 3, turn; work V-St in next ch-2 sp, ch 2, skip next dc, sc in next dc, ch 1, skip next ch-2 sp, (dc, ch 1) 4 times in next ch-3 sp, sc in next dc, ch 2, skip next ch-2 sp, work V-St in next ch-2 sp, ★ ch 1, (sc, ch 3, sc) in next ch-3 sp, ch 1, work

9

V-St in next ch-2 sp, ch 2, skip next dc, sc in next dc, ch 1, skip next ch-2 sp, (dc, ch 1) 4 times in next ch-3 sp, sc in next dc, ch 2, skip next ch-2 sp, work V-St in next ch-2 sp; repeat from ★ across to last 2 dc, skip next dc, dc in last dc: 57 sps.

Row 4: Ch 3, turn; work V-St in next ch-2 sp, skip next ch-2 sp, work Puff St in next ch-1 sp, (ch 2, work Puff St in next ch-1 sp) 4 times, skip next ch-2 sp, work V-St in next ch-2 sp, ★ skip next ch-1 sp, work (Puff St, ch 3, Puff St) in next ch-3 sp, skip next ch-1 sp, work V-St in next ch-2 sp, skip next ch-2 sp, work Puff St in next ch-1 sp, (ch 2, work Puff St in next ch-1 sp) 4 times, skip next ch-2 sp, work V-St in next ch-2 sp; repeat from ★ across to last 2 dc, skip next dc, dc in last dc: 34 sps.

Row 5: Ch 3, turn; work V-St in next ch-2 sp, ch 3, skip next ch-2 sp, sc in next ch-2 sp, ch 3, sc in next Puff St, ch 3, sc in next ch-2 sp, ch 3, skip next ch-2 sp, work V-St in next ch-2 sp, ★ ch 1, (sc, ch 3, sc) in next ch-3 sp, ch 1, work V-St in next ch-2 sp, ch 3, skip next ch-2 sp, sc in next ch-2 sp, ch 3, sc in next Puff St, ch 3, sc in next ch-2 sp, ch 3, skip next ch-2 sp, work V-St in next ch-2 sp; repeat from ★ across to last 2 dc, skip next dc, dc in last dc: 42 sps.

Row 6: Ch 3, turn; work V-St in next ch-2 sp, ch 2, dc in next ch-3 sp, ch 2, sc in next ch-3 sp, ch 3, sc in next ch-3 sp, ch 2, dc in next ch-3 sp, ch 2, work V-St in next ch-2 sp, ★ skip next ch-1 sp, work (Puff St, ch 3, Puff St) in next ch-3 sp, skip next ch-1 sp, work V-St in next ch-2 sp, ch 2, dc in next ch-3 sp, ch 2, sc in next ch-3 sp, ch 3, sc in next ch-3 sp, ch 2, dc in next ch-3 sp, ch 2, work V-St in next ch-2 sp; repeat from ★ across to last 2 dc, skip next dc, dc in last dc: 39 sps.

Rows 7-66: Repeat Rows 3-6, 15 times; do **not** finish off.

EDGING
Rnd 1: Ch 1, do **not** turn; sc in first corner; working in end of rows, work 130 sc evenly spaced across to next corner, place marker around last sc made for st placement, sc in corner; working in sps over beginning ch, work 90 sc evenly spaced across to next corner, place marker around last sc made for st placement, sc in corner; working in end of rows, work 130 sc evenly spaced across to next corner, place marker around last sc made for st placement, sc in corner; working across Row 66, work 90 sc evenly spaced across, place marker around last sc made for st placement; join with slip st to first sc: 444 sc.

Rnd 2: Ch 1, (sc, ch 3) twice in same st and in next sc, skip next 2 sc, (sc in next sc, ch 3, skip next 2 sc) twice, † (sc in next sc, ch 3) twice, skip next 2 sc, (sc in next sc, ch 3, skip next 2 sc) twice †, repeat from † to † across to next marked sc, ★ (sc, ch 3) twice in marked sc and in each of next 2 sc, skip next 2 sc, (sc in next sc, ch 3, skip next 2 sc) twice, repeat from † to † across to next marked sc; repeat from ★ 2 times **more**, (sc, ch 3) twice in last marked sc; join with slip st to first sc: 192 ch-3 sps.

Rnd 3: Slip st in first ch-3 sp, pull up a $1/2$" loop, (work Puff St in same sp, ch 3) twice, sc in next ch-3 sp, (ch 3, work Puff St) twice in next ch-3 sp, † ch 5, skip next ch-3 sp, sc in next ch-3 sp, ch 5, skip next ch-3 sp, work (Puff St, ch 3, Puff St) in next ch-3 sp †, repeat from † to † across to within one sp of next corner ch-3 sp, ★ [ch 3, sc in next ch-3 sp, (ch 3, work Puff St) twice in next ch-3 sp] twice, repeat from † to † across to within one sp of next corner ch-3 sp; repeat from ★ 2 times **more**, ch 3, sc in last ch-3 sp, ch 3; join with slip st to top of first Puff St: 156 sps.

Rnd 4: Slip st in first ch-3 sp, ch 1, (sc in same sp, ch 3) twice, (sc in next ch-3 sp, ch 3) twice, ★ (sc, ch 3) twice in next ch-3 sp, (sc in next sp, ch 3) twice; repeat from ★ around; join with slip st to first sc: 208 ch-3 sps.

Rnd 5: Slip st in first ch-3 sp, pull up a $1/2$" loop, work (Puff St, ch 3, Puff St) in same sp, ch 5, skip next ch-3 sp, sc in next ch-3 sp, ch 5, skip next ch-3 sp, ★ work (Puff St, ch 3, Puff St) in next ch-3 sp, ch 5, skip next ch-3 sp, sc in next ch-3 sp, ch 5, skip next ch-3 sp; repeat from ★ around; join with slip st to top of first Puff St: 156 sps.

Rnd 6: Slip st in first ch-3 sp, ch 1, (sc in same sp, ch 3) twice, (sc in next ch-5 sp, ch 3) twice, ★ (sc, ch 3) twice in next ch-3 sp, (sc in next ch-5 sp, ch 3) twice; repeat from ★ around; join with slip st to first sc: 208 ch-3 sps.

Rnd 7: Slip st in first ch-3 sp, pull up a $1/2$" loop, in same sp work [Puff St, (ch 3, Puff St) twice], ch 5, skip next ch-3 sp, sc in next ch-3 sp, ch 5, skip next ch-3 sp, † work (Puff St, ch 3, Puff St) in next ch-3 sp, ch 5, skip next ch-3 sp, sc in next ch-3 sp, ch 5, skip next ch-3 sp †, repeat from † to † across to next corner ch-3 sp,

★ in corner ch-3 sp work [Puff St, (ch 3, Puff St) twice], ch 5, skip next ch-3 sp, sc in next ch-3 sp, ch 5, skip next ch-3 sp, repeat from † to † across to next corner ch-3 sp; repeat from ★ 2 times **more**; join with slip st to top of first Puff St: 160 sps.

Rnd 8: Slip st in first ch-3 sp, ch 4, (dc in same sp, ch 1) 3 times, † (dc, ch 1) 4 times in next ch-3 sp, sc in next ch-5 sp, ch 3, sc in next ch-5 sp, ch 1 †, repeat from † to † across to next corner 2 ch-3 sp group, ★ (dc, ch 1) 4 times in each of next 2 ch-3 sps, sc in next ch-5 sp, ch 3, sc in next ch-5 sp, ch 1, repeat from † to † across to next corner 2 ch-3 sp group; repeat from ★ 2 times **more**; join with slip st to third ch of beginning ch-4: 328 sps.

Rnd 9: Slip st in first ch-1 sp, pull up a $1/2$" loop, work Puff St in same sp, (ch 2, work Puff St in next ch-1 sp) 7 times, sc in next ch-3 sp, † work Puff St in next ch-1 sp, (ch 2, work Puff St in next ch-1 sp) 4 times, sc in next ch-3 sp †, repeat from † to † across to next corner 9 ch-1 sp group, work Puff St in first ch-1 sp of corner group, ★ (ch 2, work Puff St in next ch-1 sp) 8 times, sc in next ch-3 sp, repeat from † to † across to next corner 9 ch-1 sp group, work Puff St in first ch-1 sp of corner group; repeat from ★ 2 times **more**, ch 2; join with slip st to top of first Puff St: 224 ch-2 sps.

Rnd 10: Slip st in first ch-2 sp, ch 7, dc in fourth ch from hook, (dc in next ch-2 sp, ch 4, dc in fourth ch from hook) 5 times, sc in next 2 ch-2 sps, ch 4, dc in fourth ch from hook, † (dc in next ch-2 sp, ch 4, dc in fourth ch from hook) twice, sc in next 2 ch-2 sps, ch 4, dc in fourth ch from hook †, repeat from † to † across working last sc in first ch-2 sp of next corner 8 ch-2 sp group, ★ (dc in next ch-2 sp, ch 4, dc in fourth ch from hook) 6 times, sc in next 2 ch-2 sps, ch 4, dc in fourth ch from hook, repeat from † to † across working last sc in first ch-2 sp of next corner 8 ch-2 sp group; repeat from ★ 2 times **more**; join with slip st to third ch of beginning ch-7, finish off.

Design by Terry Kimbrough.

1

3

14

3. LACY-SOFT LAYETTE

Shown on page 14.

Finished Size:
Layette - 9 to 12 months
Shawl - 39" square

MATERIALS

Baby Fingering Weight Yarn:
Complete Set - 17 ounces,
(480 grams, 2,625 yards)
Sacque - 4$^1/_2$ ounces,
(130 grams, 695 yards)
Bonnet and Slippers - 1$^1/_2$
ounces, (40 grams, 230 yards)
Shawl - 11 ounces,
(310 grams, 1,695 yards)
Crochet hooks, sizes D (3.25
mm) **and** F (3.75 mm) **or** sizes
needed for gauge
$^1/_4$"w Ribbon:
Complete Set - 10 yards
Sacque - 2 yards
Bonnet - 1$^1/_2$ yards
Slippers - 1$^1/_2$ yards
Shawl - 5 yards
Sewing needle and thread
Tapestry needle

GAUGE: With smaller size hook,
22 hdc and 16 rows = 4"
With larger size hook,
20 hdc and 14 rows = 4"
In pattern, 5 Cross Sts = 3$^3/_4$"
and 3 repeats = 3$^1/_4$"

To work Cross St, skip next
st, dc in next 3 sts, YO, working
around 3-dc group just made,
insert hook from **front** to **back**
in skipped st, YO and pull up a
loop even with last dc made, (YO
and draw through 2 loops on
hook) twice **(long dc made)**.

SACQUE
BODY

With larger size hook, ch 139
loosely.

Row 1: Sc in second ch from
hook and in each ch across: 138
sc.

Row 2 (Right side)**:** Ch 3
**(counts as first dc, now and
throughout)**, turn; work Cross
Sts across to last sc, dc in last sc:
34 Cross Sts.

Note: Mark last row as **right**
side.

Row 3: Ch 3, turn; work Cross
Sts across to last dc, dc in last
dc.

Rows 4 and 5: Ch 1, turn; sc
in each st across: 138 sc.

Rows 6-24: Repeat Rows 2-5,
4 times; then repeat Rows 2-4
once **more**.

Change to smaller size hook.

To sc decrease, pull up a loop
in next 2 sts, YO and draw
through all 3 loops on hook
(counts as one sc).

Row 25: Ch 1, turn; sc in first
8 sc, sc decrease, (sc in next 5
sc, sc decrease) across to last 9
sc, sc in last 9 sc; do **not** finish
off: 120 sc.

RIGHT FRONT

Row 1: Ch 2 **(counts as first hdc, now and throughout)**, turn; hdc in next 27 sc, leave remaining 92 sc unworked: 28 hdc.

Row 2 (Decrease row)**:** Ch 1, turn; hdc in next hdc and in each hdc across: 27 hdc.

Row 3: Ch 2, turn; hdc in next hdc and in each hdc across.

Rows 4-8: Repeat Rows 2 and 3 twice, then repeat Row 2 once **more**: 24 hdc.

To hdc decrease *(uses next 2 hdc)*, ★ YO, insert hook in **next** hdc, YO and pull up a loop; repeat from ★ once **more**, YO and draw through all 5 loops on hook **(counts as one hdc)**.

Row 9 (Decrease row)**:** Ch 2, turn; hdc in next hdc and in each hdc across to last 2 hdc, hdc decrease: 23 hdc.

Row 10 (Decrease row)**:** Ch 1, turn; hdc in next hdc and in each hdc across: 22 hdc.

Rows 11-16: Repeat Rows 9 and 10, 3 times: 16 hdc.

Rows 17 and 18: Ch 1, turn; hdc in next hdc and in each hdc across to last 2 hdc, hdc decrease: 12 hdc.

Finish off.

BACK

Row 1: With **right** side facing and smaller size hook, skip first 4 sc from Right Front and join yarn with slip st in next sc; ch 2, hdc in next 55 sc, leave remaining 32 sc unworked: 56 hdc.

Row 2 (Decrease row)**:** Ch 1, turn; hdc in next hdc and in each hdc across to last 2 hdc, hdc decrease: 54 hdc.

Row 3: Ch 2, turn; hdc in next hdc and in each hdc across.

Rows 4-15: Repeat Rows 2 and 3 twice; then repeat Row 2, 8 times **more**: 34 hdc.

Row 16: Ch 1, turn; hdc in next 15 hdc, hdc decrease, hdc in each hdc across to last 2 hdc, hdc decrease: 31 hdc.

Row 17: Ch 1, turn; hdc in next 13 hdc, hdc decrease, hdc in each hdc across to last 2 hdc, hdc decrease: 28 hdc.

Row 18: Ch 1, turn; hdc in next 12 hdc, hdc decrease, hdc in each hdc across to last 2 hdc, hdc decrease; finish off: 25 hdc.

LEFT FRONT

Row 1: With **right** side facing and smaller size hook, skip first 4 sc from Back and join yarn with slip st in next sc; ch 2, hdc in next sc and in each sc across: 28 hdc.

Row 2 (Decrease row)**:** Ch 2, turn; hdc in next hdc and in each hdc across to last 2 hdc, hdc decrease: 27 hdc.

Row 3: Ch 2, turn; hdc in next hdc and in each hdc across.

Rows 4-8: Repeat Rows 2 and 3 twice, then repeat Row 2 once **more**: 24 hdc.

Row 9 (Decrease row)**:** Ch 1, turn; hdc in next hdc and in each hdc across: 23 hdc.

Row 10 (Decrease row)**:** Ch 2, turn; hdc in next hdc and in each hdc across to last 2 hdc, hdc decrease: 22 hdc.

Rows 11-16: Repeat Rows 9 and 10, 3 times: 16 hdc.

Rows 17 and 18: Ch 1, turn; hdc in next hdc and in each hdc across to last 2 hdc, hdc decrease: 12 hdc.

Finish off.

SLEEVE

With larger size hook, ch 55 **loosely**.

Row 1: Sc in second ch from hook and in each ch across: 54 sc.

Row 2 (Right side)**:** Ch 3, turn; work Cross Sts across to last sc, dc in last sc: 13 Cross Sts.

Note: Mark last row as **right** side.

Row 3: Ch 3, turn; work Cross Sts across to last dc, dc in last dc.

Rows 4 and 5: Ch 1, turn; sc in each st across: 54 sc.

Rows 6-20: Repeat Rows 2-5, 3 times; then repeat Rows 2-4 once **more**.

Change to smaller size hook.

Row 21: Ch 1, turn; sc in first 3 sc, sc decrease, (sc in next 5 sc, sc decrease) across: 46 sc.

Row 22: Turn; slip st in first 3 sc, ch 2, hdc in next sc and in each sc across to last 2 sc, leave remaining sc unworked: 42 hdc.

Row 23 (Decrease row)**:** Ch 1, turn; hdc in next hdc and in each hdc across to last 2 hdc, hdc decrease: 40 hdc.

Row 24: Ch 2, turn; hdc in next hdc and in each hdc across.

Rows 25-35: Repeat Rows 23 and 24 twice; then repeat Row 23, 7 times **more**: 22 hdc.

Row 36: Ch 1, turn; hdc in next 9 hdc, hdc decrease, hdc in next 8 hdc, hdc decrease: 19 hdc.

Row 37: Ch 1, turn; (hdc in next 7 hdc, hdc decrease) twice: 16 hdc.

Row 38: Ch 1, turn; hdc in next 6 hdc, hdc decrease, hdc in next 5 hdc, hdc decrease: 13 hdc.

Row 39: Ch 1, turn; (hdc in next 4 hdc, hdc decrease) twice; finish off: 10 hdc.

Sew underarm seam, beginning at bottom of Row 1 and ending at top of Row 21.

Centering seam at underarm, sew Sleeve in place, easing to fit along raglan edges.

Repeat for second Sleeve.

FINISHING
BODY EDGING
Rnd 1: With **right** side facing and smaller size hook, join yarn with sc in hdc at center of Back neck edge *(see Joining With Sc, page 2)*; sc evenly around entire Sacque working an even number of sc; join with slip st to first sc.

Rnd 2: Ch 4, skip next sc, ★ slip st in next sc, ch 4, skip next sc; repeat from ★ around; join with slip st to first slip st.

Rnd 3: Ch 6, (slip st in next slip st, ch 6) around; join with slip st to first slip st, finish off.

Weave a one yard length of ribbon through Rnd 2 ch-4 sps along neck edge only.

SLEEVE EDGING
Rnd 1: With **right** side facing, smaller size hook, and working in free loops of beginning ch *(Fig. 1, page 2)*, join yarn with sc in any ch; sc decrease, (sc in next ch, sc decrease) around; join with slip st to first sc: 36 sc.

Rnd 2 (Eyelet rnd)**:** Ch 5 **(counts as first dc plus ch 2)**, skip next 2 sc, ★ dc in next sc, ch 2, skip next 2 sc; repeat from ★ around; join with slip st to first dc: 12 ch-2 sps.

Rnd 3: Ch 1, sc in same st, 2 sc in next ch-2 sp, (sc in next dc, 2 sc in next ch-2 sp) around; join with slip st to first sc, finish off.

Weave an 18" length of ribbon through Eyelet rnd; pull ends to gather Sleeve and tie ends in a bow.

Repeat for second Sleeve.

BONNET
BACK
With smaller size hook, ch 5; join with slip st to form a ring.

Rnd 1 (Right side)**:** Ch 2, 14 hdc in ring; join with slip st to first hdc: 15 hdc.

Note: Mark last round as **right** side.

Rnd 2: Ch 2, 2 hdc in next hdc, (hdc in next 2 hdc, 2 hdc in next hdc) 4 times, hdc in last hdc; join with slip st to first hdc: 20 hdc.

Rnd 3: Ch 1, sc in same st, ch 4, skip next hdc, ★ sc in next hdc, ch 4, skip next hdc; repeat from ★ around; join with slip st to first sc: 10 ch-4 sps.

Rnd 4: Slip st in first ch-4 sp, ch 1, 4 sc in same sp and in each ch-4 sp around; join with slip st to first sc: 40 sc.

Rnd 5: Ch 2, hdc in next 3 sc, 2 hdc in next sc, ★ hdc in next 4 sc, 2 hdc in next sc; repeat from ★ around; join with slip st to first hdc: 48 hdc.

Rnd 6: Ch 1, sc in same st, ch 5, skip next 3 hdc, ★ sc in next hdc, ch 5, skip next 3 hdc; repeat from ★ around; join with slip st to first sc: 12 ch-5 sps.

Rnd 7: Slip st in first ch-5 sp, ch 1, 5 sc in same sp and in each ch-5 sp around; join with slip st to first sc: 60 sc.

Rnd 8: Ch 2, hdc in next 3 sc, 2 hdc in next sc, ★ hdc in next 4 sc, 2 hdc in next sc; repeat from ★ around; join with slip st to first hdc: 72 hdc.

Rnd 9: Ch 2, hdc in next hdc and in each hdc around; join with slip st to first hdc.

Rnd 10: Ch 1, sc in same st, ch 5, skip next 3 hdc, ★ sc in next hdc, ch 5, skip next 3 hdc; repeat from ★ around; join with slip st to first sc: 18 ch-5 sps.

Rnd 11: Slip st in first ch-5 sp, ch 1, 5 sc in same sp and in each ch-5 sp around; join with slip st to first sc: 90 sc.

Rnd 12: Ch 1, sc in same st, 2 sc in next sc, (sc in next 18 sc, 2 sc in next sc) twice, sc in each sc around; join with slip st to first sc, do **not** finish off: 93 sc.

CROWN

Row 1: Ch 1, **turn**; sc in same st and in next 72 sc, leave remaining 20 sc unworked: 73 sc.

Row 2: Ch 1, turn; sc in each sc across.

Row 3: Ch 2, turn; hdc in next sc and in each sc across.

Rows 4-13: Ch 2, turn; hdc in next hdc and in each hdc across to last 2 hdc, hdc decrease: 63 hdc.

Rows 14-18: Ch 2, turn; hdc in next hdc and in each hdc across.

Row 19: Turn; slip st in first hdc, ★ ch 4, skip next hdc, slip st in next hdc; repeat from ★ across.

Row 20: Turn; slip st in first slip st, (ch 6, slip st in next slip st) across; do **not** finish off.

NECK EDGING

Row 1: Ch 1, do **not** turn; work 33 sc evenly spaced across end of rows; sc in next 20 sc on Back; work 33 sc evenly spaced across end of rows: 86 sc.

Row 2: Ch 1, turn; skip first sc, sc in next 2 sc, (sc decrease, sc in next sc) 10 times, sc decrease 10 times, (sc in next sc, sc decrease) across; finish off.

Fold last 4 rows of Crown to right side and tack in place.

Sew one end of a 20" length of ribbon to one corner on front of Bonnet; tie a 7" length of ribbon in a bow and sew to corner.

Repeat for second corner.

SLIPPERS
SOLE AND SIDES

With larger size hook and leaving a long end for sewing, ch 38 **loosely**; being careful not to twist ch, join with slip st to form a ring.

Rnd 1: Ch 2, hdc in next ch and in each ch around; join with slip st to first hdc: 38 hdc.

Rnd 2 (Right side)**:** Ch 2, turn; hdc in same st, 2 hdc in each of next 2 hdc, hdc in next 14 hdc, 2 hdc in each of next 5 hdc, hdc in next 14 hdc, 2 hdc in each of last 2 hdc; join with slip st to first hdc: 48 hdc.

Note: Mark last round as **right** side.

Rnds 3-6: Ch 2, turn; hdc in next hdc and in each hdc around; join with slip st to first hdc.

Rnd 7 (Eyelet rnd)**:** Ch 3, turn; skip next hdc, hdc in next hdc, (ch 1, skip next hdc, hdc in next hdc) 13 times, place marker around last hdc made for st placement, ch 1, skip next hdc, (hdc in next hdc, ch 1, skip next hdc) around; join with slip st to second ch of beginning ch-3, finish off: 24 sts and 24 ch-1 sps.

INSTEP

Row 1: With **right** side facing and larger size hook, join yarn with slip st in marked hdc; ch 2, (hdc in next ch-1 sp and in next hdc) 4 times, leave remaining sts unworked: 9 hdc.

Rows 2-4: Ch 2, turn; hdc in next hdc and in each hdc across.

Row 5: Ch 1, turn; hdc in next 6 hdc, hdc decrease: 7 hdc.

Row 6: Ch 2, turn; hdc in next hdc and in each hdc across; finish off.

Thread needle with long end and sew bottom seam. Sew Instep to Sides using 8 sts on each side of Slipper.

Beginning and ending at back of Slipper, weave a 27" length of ribbon through Eyelet rnd. Leave long ends for tying in a bow around ankle.

SHAWL

With larger size hook, ch 155 **loosely**.

Row 1: Sc in second ch from hook and in each ch across: 154 sc.

Row 2 (Right side)**:** Ch 3, turn; work Cross Sts across to last sc, dc in last sc: 38 Cross Sts.

Row 3: Ch 3, turn; work Cross Sts across to last dc, dc in last dc.

Rows 4 and 5: Ch 1, turn; sc in each st across: 154 sc.

Repeat Rows 2-5 until Shawl measures approximately 29" from beginning ch, ending by working Row 4; do **not** finish off.

EDGING

Rnd 1: Ch 1, do **not** turn; (sc, ch 1, sc) in same st; work 152 sc evenly spaced across end of rows; working in free loops of beginning ch **(Fig. 1, page 2)**, (sc, ch 1, sc) in first ch (at base of first sc), sc in each ch across to last ch, (sc, ch 1, sc) in last ch; work 152 sc evenly spaced across end of rows; working across last row, (sc, ch 1, sc) in first sc, sc in each sc across; join with slip st to first sc: 616 sc and 4 ch-1 sps.

Rnd 2: Ch 1, 2 sc in same st, (sc, ch 1, sc) in next ch-1 sp, 2 sc in next sc, sc in each sc across to within one sc of next ch-1 sp, ★ 2 sc in next sc, (sc, ch 1, sc) in next ch-1 sp, 2 sc in next sc, sc in each sc across to within one sc of next ch-1 sp; repeat from ★ around; join with slip st to first sc: 632 sc and 4 ch-1 sps.

Rnd 3 (Eyelet rnd)**:** Ch 3, dc in same st, ch 1, skip next 2 sc, (2 dc, ch 5, 2 dc) in next ch-1 sp, ch 1, ★ skip next 2 sc, (2 dc in next sc, ch 1, skip next 2 sc) across to next ch-1 sp, (2 dc, ch 5, 2 dc) in ch-1 sp, ch 1; repeat from ★ 2 times **more**, skip next 2 sc, (2 dc in next sc, ch 1, skip next 2 sc) across; join with slip st to first dc: 212 ch-1 sps and 4 ch-5 sps.

Rnd 4: Slip st in next dc and in next ch-1 sp, ch 1, sc in same sp, ch 5, (sc, ch 5, sc) in next ch-5 sp, ch 7, (sc in same sp, ch 5) twice, ★ (sc in next ch-1 sp, ch 5) across to next ch-5 sp, (sc, ch 5, sc) in ch-5 sp, ch 7, (sc in same sp, ch 5) twice; repeat from ★ 2 times **more**, sc in next ch-1 sp, (ch 5, sc in next ch-1 sp) across, ch 2, dc in first sc to form last ch-5 sp: 228 sps.

Rnds 5-13: Ch 1, sc in same sp, (ch 5, sc in next sp) around, ch 2, dc in first sc to form last ch-5 sp.

Rnd 14: Ch 1, sc in same sp, ch 5, (sc in next ch-5 sp, ch 5) around; join with slip st to first sc, finish off.

Weave a 1¼ yard length of ribbon through Eyelet rnd at each edge of Shawl; tie ends in a bow at each corner.

4. SOFT AND SWEET LAYETTE

Shown on Front Cover.

Finished Size:
Layette - 3 months
Blanket - 39" square

MATERIALS

Sport Weight Yarn:
Complete Set - 26 ounces,
(740 grams, 2,600 yards)
Sacque - $4^1/_2$ ounces,
(130 grams, 450 yards)
Bonnet and Booties -
$2^1/_2$ ounces,
(70 grams, 250 yards)
Blanket - 19 ounces,
(540 grams, 1,900 yards)
Crochet hook, size I (5.50 mm)
or size needed for gauge
Yarn needle
$^1/_4$"w Ribbon:
Complete Set - $9^1/_2$ yards
Sacque - $1^1/_4$ yards
Bonnet - $1^3/_4$ yards
Booties - 1 yard
Blanket - $5^1/_2$ yards
Ribbon roses - 2 each for Sacque
and Bonnet; 4 for Blanket
Sewing needle and thread

GAUGE: In pattern, (sc, ch 2, hdc) 5 times and 9 rows = 3"

SACQUE
BODY
Ch 54 **loosely**.

Row 1 (Right side)**:** Dc in fourth ch from hook **(3 skipped chs count as first dc, now and throughout)** and in each ch across: 52 dc.

Note: Mark last row as **right** side.

Row 2: Ch 1, turn; skip first dc, (sc, ch 2, hdc) in next dc, ★ skip next dc, (sc, ch 2, hdc) in next dc; repeat from ★ across to last 2 dc, skip next dc, sc in last dc: 26 sc and 25 ch-2 sps.

Row 3 (Increase row)**:** Ch 1, turn; 2 sc in first sc, working **behind** ch-2 sps, 3 sc in each sc across to last sc, 2 sc in last sc: 76 sc.

Row 4: Ch 1, turn; skip first sc, (sc, ch 2, hdc) in next sc, ★ skip next sc, (sc, ch 2, hdc) in next sc; repeat from ★ across to last 2 sc, skip next sc, sc in last sc: 38 sc and 37 ch-2 sps.

Row 5: Ch 1, turn; working **behind** ch-2 sps, 2 sc in each sc across: 76 sc.

Row 6: Ch 1, turn; skip first sc, (sc, ch 2, hdc) in next sc, ★ skip next sc, (sc, ch 2, hdc) in next sc; repeat from ★ across to last 2 sc, skip next sc, sc in last sc: 38 sc and 37 ch-2 sps.

Rows 7-10: Repeat Rows 3-6: 56 sc and 55 ch-2 sps.

Row 11: Ch 1, turn; working **behind** ch-2 sps, 2 sc in each of first 9 sc, skip next 11 ch-2 sps (armhole), 2 sc in each of next 18 sc, skip next 11 ch-2 sps (armhole), 2 sc in each of last 9 sc: 72 sc.

Row 12: Ch 1, turn; skip first sc, (sc, ch 2, hdc) in next sc, ★ skip next sc, (sc, ch 2, hdc) in next sc; repeat from ★ across to last 2 sc, skip next sc, sc in last sc: 36 sc and 35 ch-2 sps.

Rows 13 and 14: Repeat Rows 3 and 4: 53 sc and 52 ch-2 sps.

Rows 15-26: Repeat Rows 5 and 6, 6 times; do **not** finish off.

EDGING

Rnd 1: Ch 1, turn; 3 sc in first sc, working **behind** ch-2 sps, sc in next sc, 2 sc in each sc across to last sc, 3 sc in last sc; work 27 sc evenly spaced across end of rows; working in free loops of beginning ch *(Fig. 1, page 2)*, 3 sc in first ch, place marker around last sc made for st placement, sc in next 50 chs, 3 sc in next ch; work 27 sc evenly spaced across end of rows; join with slip st to first sc: 217 sc.

Rnd 2: Ch 1, do **not** turn; (sc, ch 2, hdc) in same st, ★ skip next sc, (sc, ch 2, hdc) in next sc; repeat from ★ around to neck edge working last (sc, ch 2, hdc) in marked sc, [skip next 2 sc, (sc, ch 2, hdc) in next sc] 17 times, skip next sc, † (sc, ch 2, hdc) in next sc, skip next sc †, repeat from † to † around; join with slip st to first sc, finish off.

SLEEVE

Rnd 1: With **right** side facing, join yarn with sc in side of first sc at underarm *(see Joining With Sc, page 2)*; sc in same st, 2 sc in side of next sc; working **behind** ch-2 sps and in unworked sc on armhole, 2 sc in each sc around; join with slip st to first sc: 24 sc.

Rnd 2: Ch 1, turn; (sc, ch 2, hdc) in same st, skip next sc, ★ (sc, ch 2, hdc) in next sc, skip next sc; repeat from ★ around; join with slip st to first sc: 12 sc and 12 ch-2 sps.

Rnd 3: Ch 1, turn; working **behind** ch-2 sps, 2 sc in same st and in each sc around; join with slip st to first sc: 24 sc.

Rnds 4-12: Repeat Rnds 2 and 3, 4 times; then repeat Rnd 2 once **more**.

Finish off.

Repeat for second Sleeve.

Weave ribbon through Row 1 on Body, working over and under two dc.

Sew a ribbon rose to each corner at neck.

BONNET
Ch 34 **loosely**.

Row 1 (Right side): Dc in fourth ch from hook and in each ch across: 32 dc.

Note: Mark last row as **right** side.

Row 2: Ch 1, turn; skip first dc, (sc, ch 2, hdc) in next dc, ★ skip next dc, (sc, ch 2, hdc) in next dc; repeat from ★ across to last 2 dc, skip next dc, sc in last dc: 16 sc and 15 ch-2 sps.

Row 3: Ch 1, turn; working **behind** ch-2 sps, 2 sc in each sc across: 32 sc.

Row 4: Ch 1, turn; skip first sc, (sc, ch 2, hdc) in next sc, ★ skip next sc, (sc, ch 2, hdc) in next sc; repeat from ★ across to last 2 sc, skip next sc, sc in last sc: 16 sc and 15 ch-2 sps.

Rows 5 and 6: Repeat Rows 3 and 4.

Row 7: Ch 1, turn; 2 sc in first sc, working **behind** ch-2 sps, 3 sc in each sc across to last sc, 2 sc in last sc: 46 sc.

Row 8: Ch 1, turn; skip first sc, (sc, ch 2, hdc) in next sc, ★ skip next sc, (sc, ch 2, hdc) in next sc; repeat from ★ across to last 2 sc, skip next sc, sc in last sc: 23 sc and 22 ch-2 sps.

Rows 9-14: Repeat Rows 3 and 4, 3 times.

Row 15: Ch 3 (counts as first **dc, now and throughout**), turn; dc in same st, working **behind** ch-2 sps, 2 dc in next sc and in each sc across: 46 dc.

Row 16: Ch 1, turn; skip first dc, (sc, ch 2, hdc) in next dc, ★ skip next dc, (sc, ch 2, hdc) in next dc; repeat from ★ across to last 2 dc, skip next dc, sc in last dc: 23 sc and 22 ch-2 sps.

Row 17: Ch 1, turn; working **behind** ch-2 sps, 2 sc in first sc and in next sc, 3 sc in each sc across to last sc, 2 sc in last sc: 66 sc.

Row 18: Ch 1, turn; skip first sc, (sc, ch 2, hdc) in next sc, ★ skip next sc, (sc, ch 2, hdc) in next sc; repeat from ★ across to last 2 sc, skip next sc, sc in last sc; do **not** finish off: 33 sc and 32 ch-2 sps.

EDGING
To decrease, pull up a loop in next 2 chs, YO and draw through all 3 loops on hook.

Ch 3, turn; (slip st in next ch-2 sp, ch 3) across to last sc, slip st in last sc; work 14 sc evenly spaced across end of rows; working in free loops of beginning ch *(Fig. 1, page 2)*, 2 sc in first ch, sc in next ch, decrease 14 times, sc in next ch, 2 sc in next ch; work 14 sc evenly spaced across end of rows; join with slip st to base of beginning ch-3, finish off.

Weave a 20" length of ribbon through Row 1, working over and under two dc. Pull ribbon ends to gather back of Bonnet slightly and tie ends in a bow.

Weave remaining ribbon through Row 15, working over and under two dc.

Sew a ribbon rose to each end of Row 15.

BOOTIES
SOLE AND SIDES
Ch 10 **loosely**.

Rnd 1 (Right side)**:** 2 Hdc in third ch from hook, hdc in next 6 chs, 5 hdc in last ch; working in free loops of beginning ch **(Fig. 1, page 2)**, hdc in next 6 chs, 2 hdc in next ch; join with slip st to top of beginning ch: 22 sts.

Note: Mark last round as **right** side.

Rnd 2: Ch 3, 2 dc in each of next 2 hdc, dc in next 6 hdc, 2 dc in each of next 5 hdc, dc in next 6 hdc, 2 dc in each of last 2 hdc, dc in same st as first dc; join with slip st to first dc: 32 dc.

Rnd 3: Ch 1, sc in Back Loop Only of same st and each dc around **(Fig. 3, page 3)**; join with slip st to **both** loops of first sc.

Rnd 4: Ch 1, **turn**; working in both loops, (sc, ch 2, hdc) in same st, skip next sc, ★ (sc, ch 2, hdc) in next sc, skip next

sc; repeat from ★ around; join with slip st to first sc: 16 sc and 16 ch-2 sps.

Rnd 5: Ch 1, turn; working **behind** ch-2 sps, 2 sc in same st and in each sc around; join with slip st to first sc, finish off: 32 sc.

INSTEP
Row 1: With **wrong** side facing, skip joining and next 6 sc and join yarn with sc in next sc **(see Joining With Sc, page 2)**; ch 2, hdc in same st, ★ skip next sc, (sc, ch 2, hdc) in next sc; repeat from ★ 6 times **more**, skip next sc, sc in next sc, leave remaining 8 sc unworked: 9 sc and 8 ch-2 sps.

Row 2: Ch 1, turn; working **behind** ch-2 sps, 2 sc in first sc and in next sc, sc in next 5 sc, 2 sc in each of last 2 sc; finish off leaving a long end for sewing: 13 sc.

Fold Row 2 in half; working through **both** loops of each stitch on **both** thicknesses, sew seam.

CUFF
Rnd 1: With **right** side facing, join yarn with slip st in same st as joining on Rnd 5 of Sides; ch 3, dc in next sc and in each sc around to Instep, dc in same st as last sc on Row 1 of Instep; working in end of rows, dc in next 2 rows, dc in seam and in next 2 rows, dc in same st as Instep joining and in each sc around; join with slip st to first dc: 22 dc.